STREET RODS

D1300533

Andrew Morland

STREET RODS

Pre '48 American rods in colour

Osprey Colour Series

Published in 1983 by Osprey Publishing Limited
12–14 Long Acre, London WC2E 9LP
Member company of the George Philip Group

© Copyright Andrew Morland 1983

This book is copyrighted under the Berne Convention.
All rights reserved. Apart from any fair dealing for the
purpose of private study, research, criticism or review,
as permitted under the Copyright Act, 1956, no part of
this publication may be reproduced, stored in a
retrieval system, or transmitted in any form or by any
means, electronic, electrical, chemical, mechanical,
optical, photocopying, recording, or otherwise, without
prior written permission. All enquiries should be
addressed to the Publishers.

British Library Cataloguing in Publication Data

Morland, Andrew
    Street rods and custom cars.—(Colour paperback)
    1. Automobiles—Customizing
    I. Title
    629.2'222   TL145

ISBN 0-85045-491-3

Captions and text by Tony Thacker
Editor Tim Parker
Designed by Martin Richards and Joy Fitzsimmons

Printed in Hong Kong

Carl 'Kasper' Kasprzyk built this '32 hiboy
roadster using a repro fibreglass body and
brand new repro chassis rails, the production
of which indicates just how big the hot rod
business is

If you had been born in the Twenties in America, had managed to survive World War 2 and had come home to Smalltown, USA, then as likely as not you'd have longed for the missing excitement. The radio was still playing Glen Miller, but he was dead and Elvis was as yet undiscovered, TV was still in its infancy and life was again sliding by as it had been before the war. The only thing that kept you sane was cars. Not new cars because there hadn't been any whilst the war effort was on but there were plenty of early Thirties Fords kicking around. These were easily souped up by dropping in a later Ford V8 and by heck they were fast. Come the weekend you'd take the ol' daily driver, white wash some numbers on the side and go dirt tracking, or hill climbing or just out looking for girls on a Saturday night. Might even do a little stop-light racing if the action was hot.

As time went by these old jalopies got a bit sophisticated. Guys started stripping the fenders off, adding a lick of paint, maybe a set of whitewalls. Elsewhere, the more mechanically minded ones were developing cylinder heads, manifolds and camshafts to make their cars go faster. Pretty soon the less inventive guys were asking the others to supply them with their hop-up parts and so the speed equipment business began.

For one reason or another those rodders, so called because they drove hot rods, stuck with their old Fords. Why not? They were cheap, plentiful and fast.

The sidevalve Ford V8 wasn't superseded until 1955 when Chevrolet introduced its overhead valve V8. Over the next decade that grew in size and power and hot rodders all over the States got busy engine swapping. They were also updating their rods with hydraulic brakes, flashes of chrome and simple paint jobs.

By the Sixties they were splitting up into different factions, some went drag racing, some went oval tracking and some stayed on the street. Today the early Thirties Ford is still the most popular base for a hot or street rod but as the sport has grown world wide so have the prices. An original, unrodded, 1932 Ford Roadster, in fair condition, if you can find one, will cost upwards of $15,000 and the work and parts needed to rod it will more than double that figure. In desperation rodders have turned to other marques, Chevrolet, Plymouth and even the British; Austins and Ford Anglias have become common sights at street rod events.

It was at several of these events where photographer Andrew Morland took most of these photographs. Some were taken at the American Street Rod Nationals where annually more than 5000 rodders gather for nearly a week of fun and games with cars. Others were taken at the Internationals held yearly at the Thruxton Circuit, England, where rodders from all over Europe come to see and talk street rods.

Tony Thacker

After consignments like this one photographer Andrew Morland could list a multitude of people who have helped him succeed. Unfortunately space and memory doesn't allow; lack of names does not indicate lack of gratitude.

Extra special thanks for aid and inspiration must, however, go to Hannah and Mike and Laurie Johnston and the organizers of the Street Rod Nats (Minnesota Street Rod Association) and the Thruxton Internationals.

Ts are still one of the cheapest and easiest cars to build through. Chassis plans for this car were featured in *Car Craft* magazine

Contents

Coupes ain't just for chickens

The sign above this '34 says it all

Here's a trick, this '35 Hudson Essex Coupe
has a '34 Terraplane grille behind which
resides a Ford Cleveland V8, automatic
gearbox and a Posi-trak limited slip axle

Model A Coupes are best when they are
chopped and dropped with bright red paint
and plenty of chrome

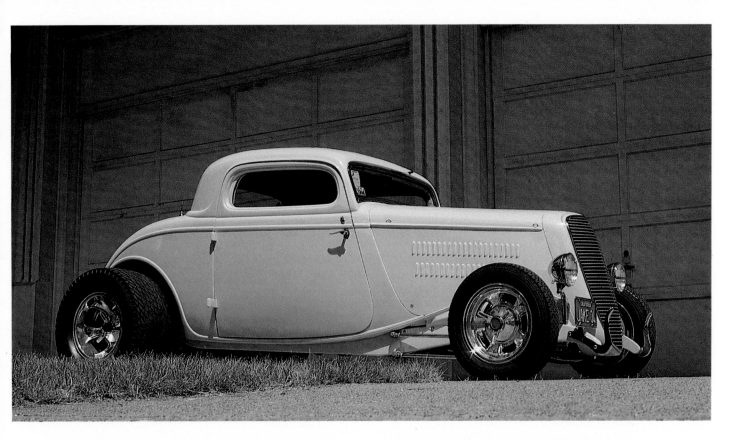

ABOVE LEFT Second to the *American Graffiti* film coupe Pete Chapouris' *California Kid* is probably the most famous rod of all. The car, a '34 Ford three-window featured in a made-for-TV movie starring Martin Sheen as the Kid. The car is Pete's daily driver and he uses it to advertise his business—Pete & Jake's Hot Rod Parts

LEFT '34 Ford five-windows are getting more popular as three-windows get rarer and dearer. This one is clean and sports CentreLine Indy Champ wheels

ABOVE The other half of Pete & Jake's is 'Jintney Jake' Jim Jacobs and this is his rendition of a '34 coupe. Fenderless hiboy styling is accentuated by the truck grille

'34 three-window coupe is rodded Sixties style
with a straight tube axle giving the front
plenty of height for weight transference and
better acceleration

This British made Jago fibreglass replica of a
'32 Ford five-window Coupe was built by
John Tredger of London. Powering the
orange great is a 3-litre Capri V6

This three-window has got to be a handful
with supercharged small-block Chevy power

Mopar magic in the form of a 1933 Plymouth
five-window Coupe

LEFT Any colour as long as it's black 'n' flames

BELOW Gold 'n' brown five-windows get ready for driving games at the Street Rod Nationals

LEFT '34 Chevy Coupes were never popular but as Ford prices rise so more and more rodders turn to General Motors products. This one has a period bumper iron protecting its drag-style Moon fuel tank

BELOW This '34 coupe has a custom grille and filled bonnet sides (no louvres)

Resto rods are street rods which look almost
original only their low stance and chrome
wheels belie the fact that modern mechanics
reside beneath the paint

22

Another prime example of the resto style

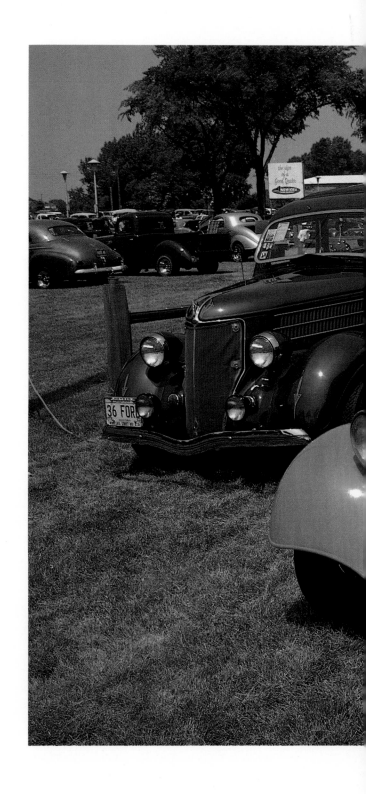

Two more resto rods, a '34 coupe in the foreground and behind it a '36 sedan

24

Restored to almost original condition, only
the candy paint, mag wheels and dropped
headlamp bar indicate that this is a rodded
'32

Now that's a hot rod. Open wheels support a
chopped and channelled body and a big
blown Chrysler Hemi engine

Pickups and panels

This '34 Ford Pickup has numerous Fifties touches like the chrome reverse rims, whitewall tyres and front nerf (bumper) bars

29

'39 Ford Pickup is built like an outhouse
with chrome reverse rims on tandem axles

This wild C-cab has an unusual engine in the
form of a supercharged small-block Ford V8

Jim Sappenfield from St Paul, Minnesota, chopped and channelled this 1938 Willys Pickup 5 inches and fitted a four cylinder, 2-litre Pinto engine which returns 31 mpg

Panel vans are hard to chop because of all
that flat sheet metal in the side. Nevertheless
Rob Juetten of White Bear Lake, Michigan,
hacked 3 inches out of his '40 Ford.
Underneath the bright yellow paint resides a
Ford 302 ci engine on an original chassis
with Chevy Nova suspension

34

LEFT Chopped '28 Model A Ford Pickup is very Eighties with its smoothed out lines and colour coded wire wheels and interior

RIGHT '33 Ford Sedan Deliveries are very rare indeed. This one looks old but has modern wheels fitted with early hub caps and the chassis is right up to date with four-link suspension

BELOW Chrome wire wheels give the resto look to this '37 Chevy Panel

35

RIGHT A '40 Ford Sedan Delivery leads a '36 Chevy on the way to the Street Rod Nationals

BELOW Two tone '39 Chevrolet Panel Van looks pretty stock from the outside but you can bet your life there is a late model small-block under the hood

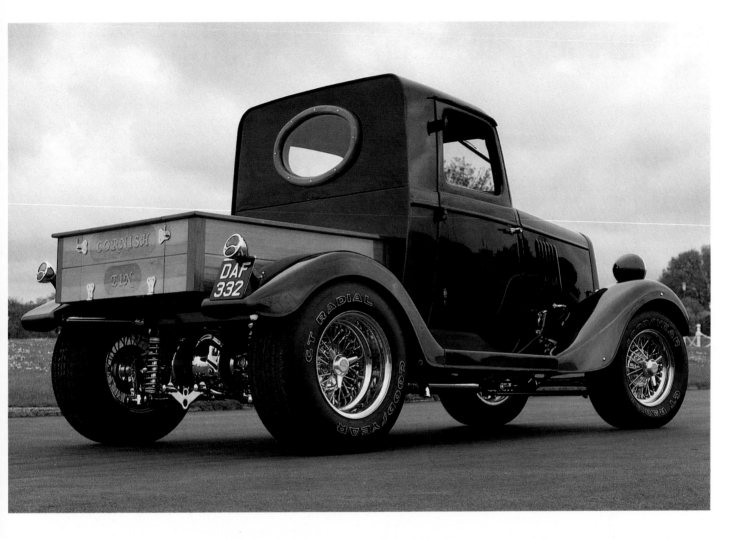

LEFT Dick Fravert has certainly chopped this '38 Ford about, fitting a '32 grille shell and discarding the bonnet to expose a much modified small-block Chevy. Bored out to 331 ci this hot motor has been blueprinted, balanced and fitted with polished and ported heads. Its output is now in the region of 600 bhp

ABOVE This chrome and gold plated 1934 Ford Model Y Pickup was built by Tony Andrews of Plymouth, England. Originally made from a sedan by a Cornish conversion company the stock frame retaining the original I-beam front axle, now features a 215 ci Rover V8, automatic gearbox and Jaguar E type independent rear suspension

European invasion

This 1952 Ford Popular was a £10 wreck when Bristol boy Richard Roberts bought it. Many hours, much money, a Rover V8, a Borg-Warner box and a Jaguar S type axle went into its construction. Saab metallic brown and Citroën gold complement the slot mags

John Fern of Hastings, Nebraska, painted
this four-door 1948 Austin Porsche Fern
Green and called it *Watsit*. A new, home
built, chassis with tube axle rides on twelve
spoke magnesium wheels up front and five-
spokers in back. The original side valve
engine has been ousted in favour of a 153 ci
four cylinder Chevy engine, Powerglide
transmission and a Chevy Vega back axle

LEFT An export Anglia, recognized by its three-hole grille has non stock headlamps and indicators plus a very suspicious looking air scoop

BELOW Another Anglia exported to America sports widened wings to cover its huge mag wheels, running boards and strange front-end treatment with quad headlights

LEFT Another four-door Austin is this one owned by Bruce Sapp called *Coffee & Cream*. Riding high on a Corvette rear axle and Corvair front axle this car is powered by a 375 bhp 350 ci Chevy. Special features include a tilt steering column and a one piece, tilting bonnet

BELOW Originally built by Rod Gazeley with a Triumph six-pot, then fitted with a Rover V8 by Alan Mills, this 1936 Morris 10 is now owned by Tim Pratt. It is painted Ford Jupiter Red with black wings and is fitted with Appliance wire mags

Clean 'n' green are the only words to describe Bill Shoquist's '48 Anglia. Riding on massive McReary 33 × 13 × 15 in. tyres and CentreLine wheels this mean greenie is propelled by a 550 bhp 350 ci Chevy V8 with 11:1 compression ratio. The inside is also immaculate being trimmed in tuck 'n' roll style saddle tan vinyl with power windows, electric door locks, tilt column and a B & M shifter

Photographed at the Thruxton Internationals was Mike Perry's Fiat Topolino. Mike, from Whitney in Oxfordshire, made his own tubular space frame with Triumph Vitesse front suspension. The rest of the running gear, from engine through back axle, came from a Mk II Ford GT 1600 crossflow

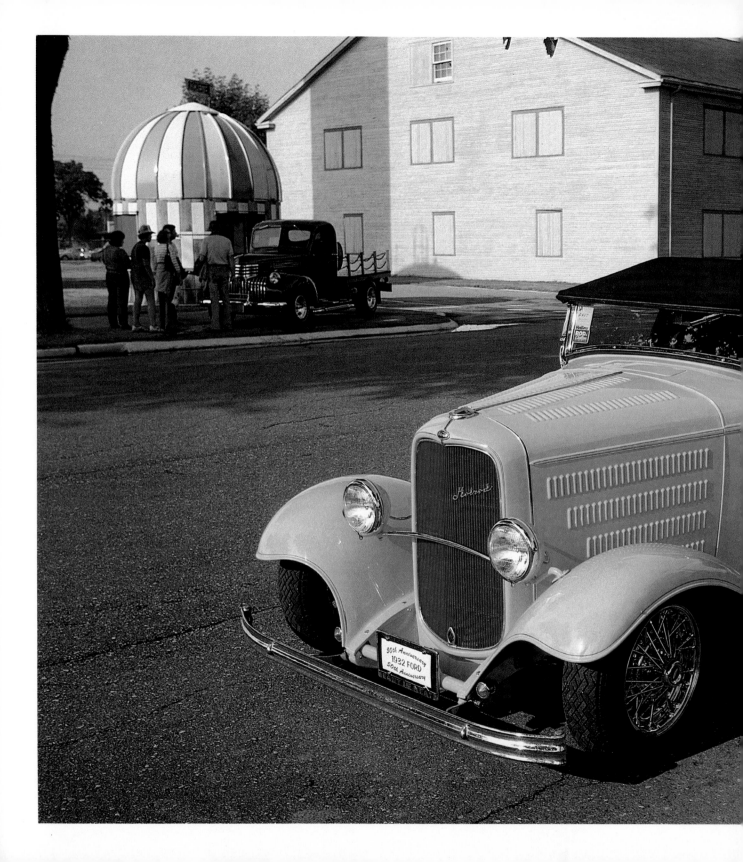

Rag tops

Chrome yellow paint, chrome wire wheels
and plenty of louvres a street rod make, as
the grille ornament on this '32 Ford Roadster
confirms

LEFT '40 Ford Convertible is red-y

BELOW, LEFT AND RIGHT A 327 ci Chevy V8
powers Bill's 1936 Ford Cabriolet

Street rodders doing what they do best,
sitting by their cars, drinking some suds,
soaking the sun and watching the action

ABOVE Say hot rod, say it loud and say it
with flames and pin stripes and say, it's a '32
Chevy Roadster Pickup

ABOVE LEFT Rag top roadsters come in all
colours

LEFT Fifties style '32 hiboy roadster has
Moon caps and matching Mooneyes
headlamp covers

This hot rod line-up includes a '32 Ford
Roadster out front, a blown 'n' blue '34
coupe and a '39 Chevy Coupe

Fat fendered friends

A classic '39 Ford De Luxe Coupe

Chopped '40 Chevy Coupe

Ain't no ride like a low ride, especially when it's a chopped '48 Chevy Fleetline

RIGHT 1940 Pontiac Coupe jammin' between
a truck and a T-bucket

BELOW '37 Ford Coupe hauls ass in the
Minnesota heat. The driver even has the
screen wound out for a little early air
conditioning

ABOVE LEFT '40 Ford Coupe rides on Western wires

ABOVE '47 Ford Coupe with fender skirts and Appleton spotlights has that Fifties high school look

LEFT A 1940 Ford De Luxe Coupe

FOLLOWING PAGE '36 Pontiac out front and a '36 Pontiac out back as a trailer

Big blown Willys Coupe spent its adolescence
on the drag strip. It's now on the street
looking just as tough as ever. Notice the
matching flames inside the flip front

Another line up, this time it's a flamed '37
Ford, a '34 Dodge and a Chevy Truck

ABOVE '41 Ford Coupe runs drilled nerf bars instead of the original bumpers

LEFT '48 Pontiac came with acres of chrome but a hot rodder added the flames and louvres

This resto '37 Chevy, complete with spare
wheel now has small-block power

Tom Held of Iowa built this '39 Chevy in 1965 for drag racing but with a lot of help from the Shade Tree Street Rod Club it was back on the road with Camaro Z28 power for the Street Rod Nats

ABOVE Jake Moran, SE divisional director of
the National Street Rod Association drives
this oh so low '38 Lincoln Zephyr

RIGHT This '41 Oldsmobile has been
customized with stacked quad headlights

74

OPPOSITE PAGE Bob Huff found his Family
Jewel, this '40 Willys, stored in a barn. It
took him two years to persuade the farmer
owner to sell. Since then he has rebuilt it
dropping in a 427 ci Chevy Rat motor which,
on its first time out, pushed the car to an 8.6,
84 mph run over an eight mile

BELOW The '37 Willys is an unusual car to
rod but this candy red four-door looks good

All street rods start their second life at the
rust removal plant

'40 Ford Sedan belongs to John 'Wings' Thoresen

ABOVE Another '40 sedan, this one with matching trailer sits in the sun at St Paul, Minnesota

LEFT A flip-front with its wild paint makes this one special street rod

Sedans

Model As are everywhere leading the parade

This Model A has all the accessories
including CB and side curtains

Hudsons are rare, Hudson street rods are
even rarer. This one belongs to Jack Smith of
Manitoba

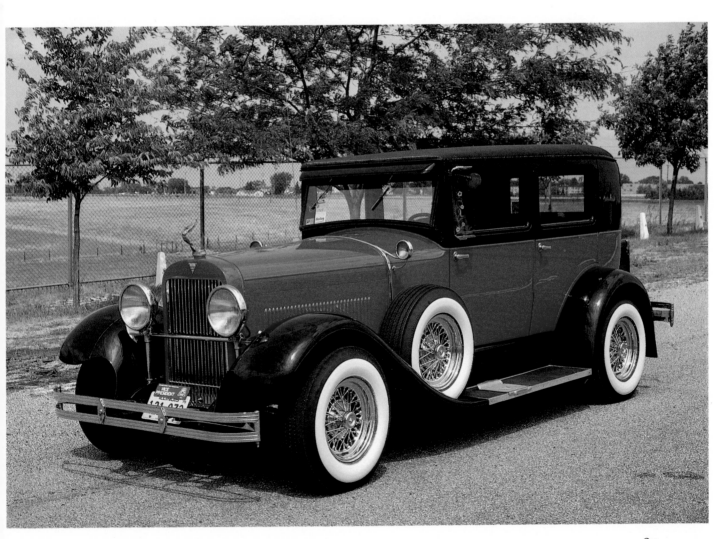

LEFT 1-LOW-A is the licence plate of this Minnesota chopped A-bone

BELOW How's this for a parts chaser? Pete & Jake's Hot Rod parts shop use this '29 Model A Pickup to do just that

ABOVE Gary Bohwart's '34 Tudor has original suspension with four-bar links, 350 ci Chevy power and a black velour interior. Starwire wheels and Ford bright red paint add that hot rod sparkle

ABOVE LEFT As hot rodders get older they, like everybody else, get families so why not take the whole crew street rodding in a four-door

LEFT Chopped model A with fadeaway paint has '32 Ford grille shell—a common rodders' trick for Model A owners

As it was never sold in the US the British Model Y is a rare street rod. This one, however, is an American made fibreglass replica built by Dwight Bond of Gibbon Fibreglass Reproductions using a 1937 60 bhp flathead Ford V8 with a Corvette four-speed gearbox and a Datsun rear axle

90

RIGHT A '32 Tudor Sedan out on the road where street rods should be

BELOW This '31 Chevy four-door is of the new breed of street rods—non Ford and very practical for the family rodder

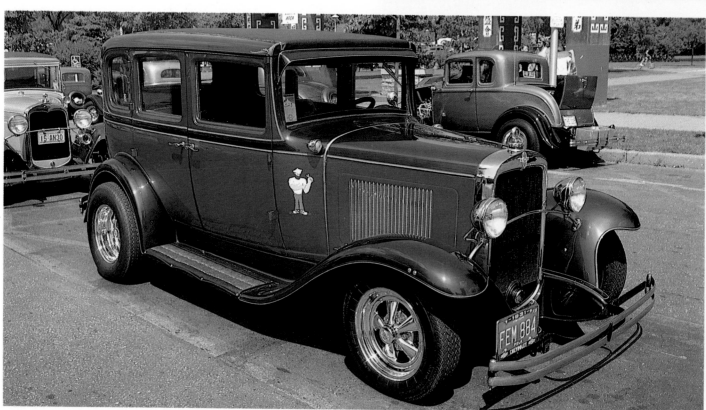

BELOW Low 'n' slow is the only way to go, especially when you drive a '41 Buick lowrider

LEFT A 1936 Ford

BELOW The '34 Chevrolet was their first
model without louvres in the bonnet sides
but the padded running boards on this street
rod are definitely not stock

RIGHT The Victoria was Ford's idea of a 2+2 coupe—this one is a '31 Model A

BELOW This guy wanted to be different so he rodded a '34 Chrysler four-door

This kandy koloured, tangerine flake, streamline baby of a '34 Ford Tudor belongs to Richard and Vivian Temple of Chicago. A 350 ci Chevy powers this XK-E steered, Vette suspended sedan

If you're gonna tow a trailer then tow a good
one. This one used to be a fairground dodgem

The owner of this '34 Fordor knows how to
nail it

No show without go

T-buckets became popular after the Sixties
TV show *77 Sunset Strip* but their
impracticality for long distance driving has
reduced their numbers

This '23 T with turtle deck is styled after the dirt track roadsters of the Forties. Blown Chevy provides the power

RIGHT Scott Ellis wowed 'em with his weedburnin' *Low Blow*. Wild T-bucket started a new trend for over the top Ts

BELOW A trick T is this '27 model built onto a VW floorpan

The ubiquitous Jaguar independent rear
suspension with Salisbury Powrlok
differential, inboard discs and adjustable coil
overs

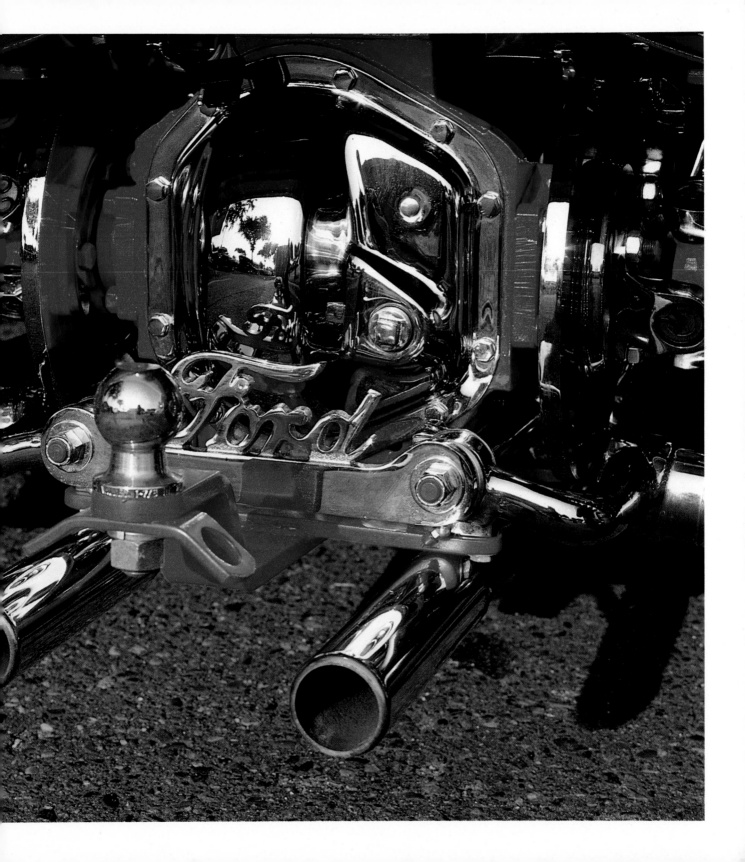

RIGHT Pip Biddlecombe of Ower, Hampshire, proved how low one can go when he built this British *Low Blow* look-alike and called it *Infinitee*. A supercharged 428 ci Pontiac blows the dust away at the Thruxton Internationals

BELOW Twin turboed Chevy powers Kollofski's wild '33 Willys

This rather dated '34 sedan has a '32 grille
shell and Chrysler hemi power

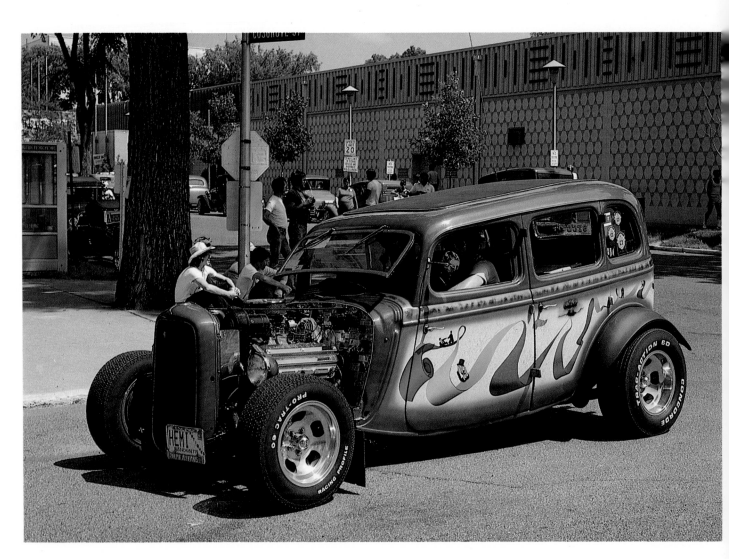

Rodders don't usually do this sort of thing
now but this was a four-door Graham sedan
which owner Mark Madson has reworked into
a two-door. 427 cubic inches of Chevy,
developing 600 bhp, power this odd rod

ABOVE Pip Biddlecombe's other car is this
chopped Austin Ruby. Its supercharged $2\frac{1}{2}$
litre Daimler (hemi) V8 has taken it into the
13 second bracket on the drag strip with
speeds over 100 mph. Pip also drives the car
on the road

LEFT Room for one more on top

RIGHT Perhaps the most powerful sounding words in the hot rodder's vocabulary—blown big-block

BELOW Ford invented the T but Chevy builds the engines

Two more Ts—two more Chevys

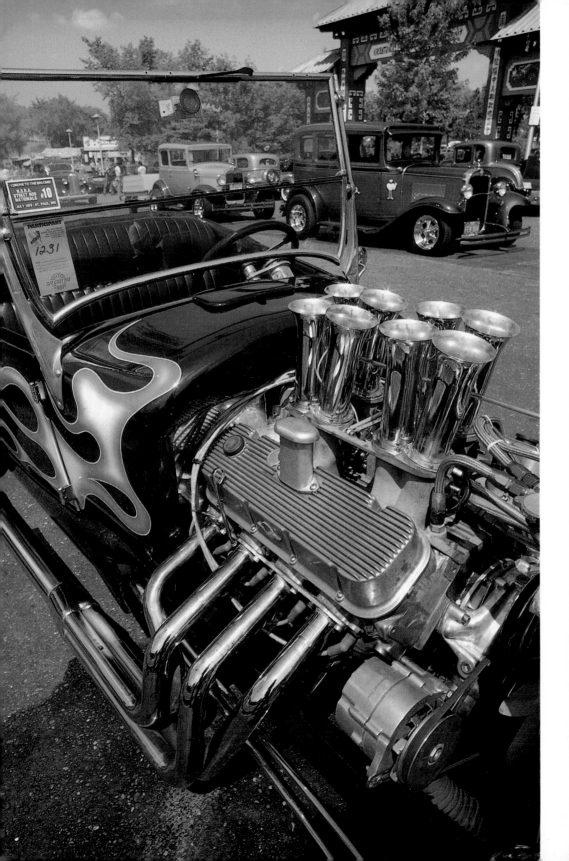

FAR LEFT Injection is fine but I'd rather be blown

LEFT A beautiful blown B

Slick licks and painting tricks

Candy stripes are achieved by first applying a white ground coat, taping out the white lines and then overspraying these with various candy colours before removing tape

Seventies style trick paint explored every avenue. Masking tape, stencils and plenty of different coloured candies are used to create this

LEFT Fadeaway jobs look easy but a perfect result is difficult to achieve. Tom McMullen's '32 tub was painted white first and then oversprayed with yellow through red to brown each time leaving a portion of the previous colour uncovered

BELOW AND FOLLOWING TWO PAGES No one knows exactly who had the first flame paint job but whoever he was he started a trend which has lasted for 40 years and has never gone out of style. They can be any shape, any colour, but the classic combination is red and yellow flames with a white pinstripe on a black car. The effect is achieved by applying first a base colour, dependent upon what colour flames you want, and then taping out the shape of the flames. This area is then oversprayed with the flame colours chosen. After that has dried it is masked over and the rest of the car is sprayed. Remove the masking and you have flames. Usually a pinstripe is added to disguise the join between the flames and the overall colour

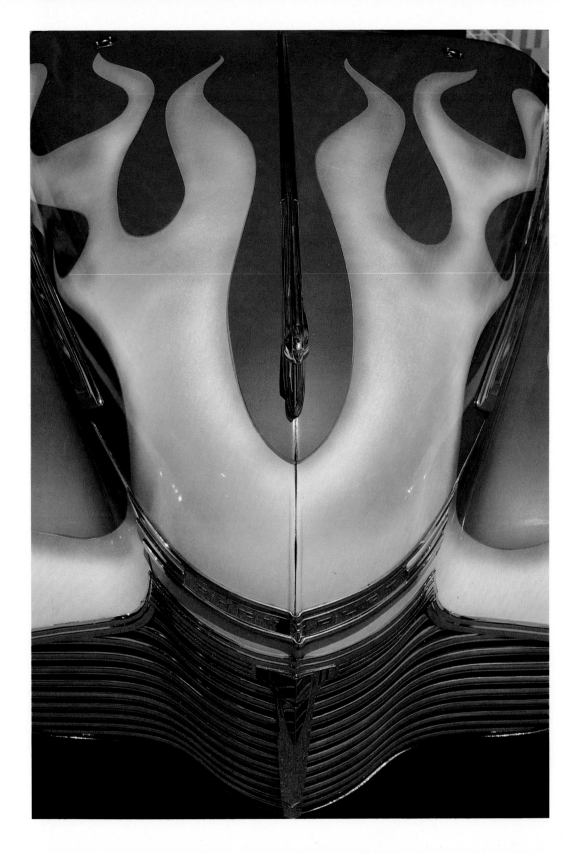

Candy colours are translucent tinters
sprayed over a gold, silver, copper or white
base. Here gold candy is oversprayed with
red to give another type of flame effect

ABOVE Metalflake has been around since the early Sixties but can still look effective. In this case the whole car would be painted in silver flake (tiny particles of anodized aluminium suspended in clear lacquer). Next the shapes are taped out using $\frac{1}{4}$in. masking tape. Then each area is sprayed in a different candy colour. When that is dry the whole patterned area is masked off whilst the rest of the car is sprayed red. Subsequent coats of clear lacquer will protect the surface

FOLLOWING PAGE Big murals like the *Sedan Wars* are out now, but small hand-painted or air-brushed cartoons characterizing the car are becoming more popular